The Harbour of Contentment

PATIENCE STRONG

The Harbour of Contentment

Off to my treasure isle of dreams I
sailed on the morning tide—with only
my hopes for compasses and only my
star to guide ... Searching for happiness
I called at many a far strange port—
then on I sailed, unsatisfied, for I knew
not what I sought.

Over the oceans of the years I
travelled but never found—the lost
horizon; so sick at heart I turned my
ship around—towards the place I had
started from; to that haven of rest I
went—home on the flow of the evening
tide to the harbour of content—there
to discover what I had wandered round
the world to find. It was there all the
time awaiting me: contentment and
peace of mind.

Sufficient

No longer will I strive and strain to be—
relieved from illness and adversity. No longer
will I offer anxious prayers—for release from
pains and worldly cares.

To come into the Presence must suffice—
of Him who holds the pearl beyond all price.
To turn to Him whose touch can heal and bless
—must be sufficient for my helplessness ... He
knows my need. My trouble He can see. Come,
Lord, and lay Thy healing hands on me.

There was a Time

There was a time when we two walked enchanted
in a land of dreams. Gay, romantic and in
love we built our hopes and wove our schemes
... Lost to the world, we trod on air and every-
thing was marvellous. The future was a magic
gate. The earth, we thought, was made for us.

Then we talked the sweetest nonsense.
Paradise was in a kiss.
We were young and life was heaven.
How, then, did we come to this? Now we talk
of bills and boilers and discuss the price of
things. What's become of all the rapture? Time,
it seems, has clipped our wings.

But we knew it had to happen. It's the
way that we are made. Love can't live amongst
the clouds. The music dies, the colours fade ...
But something comes as compensation when
we look around and see—Another sort of
happiness: the joy of home and family.

The Soloist

Alone he sang his song—from dawn to
dusk, all day. Where were the other
birds? It seemed they'd flown away, and
left him there to make his own sweet
melody—hidden in the bloom of the
lilac tree.

I worked with rake and spade until
the sun had gone—and still that lovely
thrush went singing blithely on ... Quite
flattered did I feel that he for me should
sing—when all the sky he had in which to
have his fling.

Light failed. A star came out, and
the performance stopped—as if across a
stage a curtain had been dropped—The
show was over now. A silence fell—and
then—there came two last soft notes
that sounded like—Amen.

Verges

Lovely are the verges of the lanes in summertide—
with Queen Ann's Lace with buttercups and daisies
golden-eyed ... making glowing patterns like a rich
embroidery—laid between the hedges and the roads for

all to see ... But seldom do we stop to look as hurriedly we pass—heedless of the simple beauty in the wayside grass. So it is with living as we rush from day to day—missing in our haste what God has planted by the way.

Try Praying

When life is looking black to you—Try praying. When you are wondering what to do—Try saying—a prayer aloud or silently. In moments of extremity— Prayer changes things as you will see. Try praying.

When grief and losses you must bear —Try making—a quiet moment for a prayer and taking—Your troubled heart to Him who knows—your wounds, your worries and your woes. And let His peace around you close. Try praying.

Once Again

Once again the harvest: Rye, barley,
oats and wheat. The everlasting miracle.
The cycle is complete ... the seed in spring
or autumn sown has ripened into grain.
Gold and brown the corn is glowing.
Harvest time again.

There's a quiet holiness about a field
that stands—ready for the reaping by
machine or human hands ... reverence the
earth as part of God's eternal plan. Feed
it, love it—save it from rapacity of man.

Reflections in a Wayside Church

I cannot bear to leave this place, this
sanctuary of peace and grace—where altar
flower and candle flame seem to breathe
the Holy Name.

He whose beauty drew me in—from
the world of strife and sin—drives me out
into the street—my task to do and to
complete.

I'd love to linger here alone—to
touch the cool and hallowed stone—that
gives me strength to wait and trust. I long
to stay, but go I must.

Your Blessings

Though you may be passing through a
dark and anxious time, smile and keep
your courage, for surrender is a crime.
Gratitude works magic, like the waving
of a wand. Lift your eyes above the
shadows to the world beyond.

With a glad and grateful heart, you'll
take a different view. Think of all the
benefits that Fate has showered on you.
Do not dwell upon misfortunes and the
tears you've shed; count your blessings,
drop your cares, and count your joys
instead.

So when in the morning you awake
to greet the day, do this little sum before
you go upon your way. Add up all your
blessings, past and present, great and
small; you will find that Life is not so
empty, after all.

A Beautiful Christmas

The beauty of Christmas is in its simplicity:
God in a stable, a mere human mite ...
Lord of the universe, clothed in humility—
King of the cosmos, the Life and the Light.

Make then your Christmas a time of
austerity. Feed on the bread of the truth of the
Word: on this great mystery pondering quietly.
Through all the turmoil let angels be heard ...
Sanctify Christmas. The world shut away. Make
it a simple and beautiful day.

Left Alone

You cannot see the way to go when first you're
left alone. Left to face the world and fight your
battles on your own ... You cannot understand
why such a thing should come to you. The path
ahead is hidden and the future veiled from view.

You can't imagine life without that dear
one somewhere there: the good companion of
your heart, the one who used to share—the bad
times and the happy times, the laughter and the
tears—in whom you trusted and confided all
your hopes and fears.

But do not think that no one else has
borne as much as you. Some have many years
together—others just a few. There must be a
parting. One must go and one must stay. One is
taken—one is left. It happens every day.

Bitter or Better

A bitter day or a better day. Which is it to be? A shining day or a whining day. Gloom or gaiety ... A day for chewing grievances, poisoning the blood. A day to look for something good or wallow in the mud.

A day for peace and quiet or for argument. A day to stir up trouble or to be content ... A day for turning discord into harmony. A bitter day, a better day. Which is it to be?

Over the Gate

If between the apple orchards up the hill
you go—you will find a gate that's chained
and locked—and rightly so ... Climb it.
None will question if you've come just
for the joy of seeing bluebells, not to pick,
to plunder or destroy.

Once you're over, dumb you're
struck and spellbound there you stand.
The gate that looked forbidding was the
gate to fairyland ... Half afraid, you
hesitate. It's all so still and strange—
that lake of blueness flowing out as
far as eye can range.

The path I've often wandered but
the end I've never found—for I felt a
Presence there and it was holy ground.
Not for me this ecstasy. I'd come back
later on—when the blue had faded and
the mystery had gone.

Harmony

Let us work for Harmony in every walk of life;
harmony instead of discord, jealousy and strife;
if we live in harmony, no jarring note destroys
peace of mind—relationships, and all our precious
joys.

Harmony of voices. Let no ugly sound be
heard—bickering or bitterness, the shrill and
angry word; may the voices in the house be
soothing and refined; quiet and happy, saying
only what is good and kind.

Harmony throughout the world. Oh, may
we live to see—Christ's own Kingdom. Not a
dream but a Reality. Every nation in the world
united, and yet free—working out their destinies
in perfect harmony.

Piling Up

Feather-light the snowflakes fall and melt upon
your face. Fairylike they flutter down like
wisps of dainty lace ... They seem to have no
weight, no substance or solidity—yet sometimes
on the widely spreading branches of a tree—
they form a load too heavy for a straining
bough to take—and underneath the crushing
burden it will bend and break.

Like the snowflakes heaped upon the
branches of the tree—troubles pile up on your
mind until eventually—something breaks inside
you underneath the leaden weight. So don't let
worries weigh you down or cares accumulate.
Deal with every problem as you meet it on the
way. Carry only what you have the strength
for, day by day.

Somewhere to Sit in the Sunshine

Somewhere to sit in the sunshine, That's what the old folks love. Somewhere to rest and be thankful—when there's a blue sky above—Feeling the warmth on their faces—just like a loving caress—bathed in the bliss of the moment—purring with happiness.

A seat in a park or a garden—a seat in a street or a square—A seat by a church or a bus-stop—a seat in the sun anywhere—is heaven—or something quite near it. A personal blessing it seems—to bask in the glow and the glory—alone with their thoughts and their dreams—or having a word with a stranger—a casual, impersonal chat—discussing the whims of the weather—talking of this and of that ... That's all they want when it's finished—and life's last desires fade away—Somewhere to sit in the sunshine—enjoying the end of the day.